Going Through the Wilderness

Going Through the Wilderness
Copyright © 2026 Lupita Solorio

Published by Planted Streams Media
Corona, CA

ISBN: 979-8-9939487-0-6

Cover design by Louis Bauder
Printed in the United States of America

Going Through the Wilderness

A Journey About Reflection and Hope

By: Lupita Solorio

PLANTED STREAMS
MEDIA

Contents

Introduction

My hope is that this book helps you to navigate through a difficult season in your life. All I seek to do is share what I learned in my experience so that it may help you because there is power in testimony.

If He allows something difficult to happen in our lives it is not to harm us, it is to grow us. He is a good, good Father and once we truly understand that in our heart then we can move forward.

When we go through very difficult situations it is easy to assume that God is mad at us or we might even get mad at Him, and shake our fist to heaven wondering why He would ever allow this to happen. Sometimes God answers as he did to Job

"Where were you when I laid the earth's foundation? Tell me, if you understand. Who marked off its dimensions? Surely you know! Who stretched a measuring line across it? On what were its footings set, or who laid its cornerstone—while the morning stars sang together and all the angels shouted for joy? (Job 38: 4-7 NIV)

While God is not only truth-filled but IS truth himself and unable of lying, He is also our loving Abba Father who draws near in our times of trouble. God IS love. He tenderly is with us when our heart is broken. He knows how to approach each one of us.

The troubles we face in life can come because of the brokenness of the world, and can be circumstantial. Other times, they are the result of dumb decisions we make as humans and then we blame others or God for. But not always. Because the Spirit of God is the one who leads us to the wilderness to test us and shape our character.

Just "Then Jesus was led by the Spirit into the wilderness to be tempted by the devil." (Matthew 4:1 NIV)

Why would the Spirit of God lead Jesus to the wilderness to be tempted by the devil? Because it was part of his processing. Even Jesus who was fully God and fully man got processed this way.

When the Spirit of God allows us to get into times in the wilderness there is always a purpose and hope on the other side. He is getting us ready for a next season.

Just as God did with the Israelites when he said "Then the LORD said to Moses, 'Go to Pharaoh and say to him,

'This is what the LORD, the God of the Hebrews, says: "Let my people go, so that they may worship me."

(Exodus 9:1 NIV) God wanted his people to go to the wilderness to worship him. They would worship in the wilderness before entering the promise land.

God first sends us to the wilderness to prepare us for what's next; His intention was never for His people to go back to the slavery of Egypt after worshipping in the desert, instead it was to take them to their promise land after.

While in the wilderness, worship him.

May this book comfort you and lead you through navigating out of a season of wilderness. May you encounter God in this time as you read and I hope that it connects you deeper with your Abba Father and that He will show you your next destination.
What is on the other side of this season, because if it's not good yet, He is not done writing your story.

What I Learned in the Wilderness:

"In this world you will have trouble. But take heart! I have overcome the world." (John 16:33b NIV)

Jesus assures us this so that we know that no matter the challenge, this too shall pass!

While we are in the wilderness, overcoming it may seem impossible, like you will be in the wilderness for life, but you don't have to be.

At times God almighty in His sovereignty will allow us to go through wilderness seasons but it's not for our harm but rather for our good. It is mind boggling to our human capacity that these challenges will ever be beneficial for us but remember God's word:
"'For my thoughts are not your thoughts, neither are your ways my ways,' declares the LORD. 'As the heavens are higher than the earth, so are my ways than your ways and my thoughts than your thoughts." (Isaiah 55:8-9 NIV)

So, what is the wilderness? What is the purpose of the wilderness?
God tells us exactly the purpose of the wilderness.

"Remember that the LORD your God led you on the entire journey these forty years in the wilderness, so that he might humble you and test you to know what was in your heart, whether or not you would keep his commands." (Deuteronomy 8:2 CSB)

To humble us and test what is in our hearts?
No wonder the wilderness is hard!

First, I'll talk about my wilderness. There are not many details that need to be said because the wilderness is not about what happens to us, but what we learn while we are in it that allows us to overcome it and get to the other side. My husband and I lost our daughter, Elah. She went to be with Jesus just two short days after her birth. Elah was our third born child, and prior to me delivering her at 31 weeks pregnant, we had absolutely no idea there was anything wrong with the pregnancy. It was an utterly unexpected shock, and after her loss, we entered into the wilderness.

How could we deal with something so devastating? By drawing near to God, and thankfully by His Grace, that's exactly what we did.

God used my husband with his sensibility to the Holy Spirit and obedience to tell me that I needed to start journaling, to let everything out on paper, to process

my emotions. I have not always been the best at dealing with emotions.
That's part of what the wilderness taught me actually, how to be healthier in that sense.

Anyhow, I went and bought a journal and decided it was a good idea because I had enjoyed writing when I was in school. I remembered how nice it always felt to write about anything, although I had just done it for assignments. I also had a bit of journaling practice because I previously used the "5 Minute Journal" by UJ Ramdas and Alex Iconn. This journal was a practice that started me off well since it was a very short exercise with prompts. This made it easier to practice as I didn't have to think much about what to write.

Additionally, I completed "The Purpose Driven Life Journal" by Rick Warren, which dove deeper into emotions and my spiritual life. I am so thankful that I had access to both of these resources before entering into my own wilderness season.

Journaling independently during my wilderness season was different. Here were no assignments, no prompts - just very raw, painful emotions to be thrown at an absolutely blank page. The good thing is that I knew I wasn't doing it alone. I could feel the Spirit of God with me, in a more palpable way than I had ever felt before. This is when His word started coming to life. I understood passages with my whole being and not just with my mind. For example, when He tells us "The LORD is close to the brokenhearted; he saves those crushed in spirit." (Psalms 34:18 CSB) That's exactly the reality that I was living in those moments. God knew my broken heart and He was close to me.

After I dropped off my oldest son in 3rd grade and my youngest son in kindergarten, I would walk to my car, still in pain and recovering physically from giving birth; I would close the door to my car and it felt like a safe place. My own little world in which I could cry, worship, write, do anything that I needed to do. I would pull out my journal and start writing in the school's parking lot.

Through the journaling, God showed me so many things that I took as lessons for myself and all I want to do in this simple writing is to share those lessons to the best of my ability. What I learned in my wilderness.

Lesson 1:

God is With Us in the Wilderness

God does not leave you alone in the wilderness. Just as Jesus told His disciples, "Nevertheless, I am telling you the truth. It is for your benefit that I go away, because if I don't go away the Counselor will not come to you. If I go, I will send him to you." (John 16:7 CSB) Well, the Counselor sure showed up for me. The Holy Spirit was with me and I know that every prayer, every emotion, every cry, everything; I was living it with the Living God. When we get close to Him, He sure is there with us which is exactly what His word shows us.

But like I said, the word was becoming alive for the first time in my life. "Draw near to God, and he will draw near to you." (James 4:8a CSB) I needed God so desperately and I wanted to be with Him so much, and He drew near to me.

The fact that God is with us, is written throughout scripture and the wilderness proved this to me. Oftentimes we think something is a God problem but it is always an "us" problem. Of course, we never realize that until a catastrophe shakes our world and forces us to take a closer look at ourselves. I know this to be true because that's exactly what I experienced in losing Elah. Even though I loved God and had been actively attending church for over 10 years, hosted a life group in my home for 5 years, and even served at church, I still somehow felt disconnected. I felt I wasn't fully experiencing God how He wants us to or the way my soul was craving. I knew that His word said "You will seek me and find me when you search for me with all of your heart." (Jeremiah 29:13 CSB). "All of your heart" are the key words! Looking back, prior to this wilderness I knew my connection to God was strong but not as strong as it could be.

Was I not seeking him with all of my heart? Many of us can ask this question in our deepest self-analysis and if we find ourselves asking, it's probably because something needs to change.

I know that for me there were too many things of this world getting in the way of my pursuit of God and seeking Him with all of my heart. I was doing the opposite of "But seek first the kingdom of God and his righteousness, and all these things will be provided for you." (Matthew 6:33 CSB). I was too consumed by the pursuit that the world offers, especially in a materialistic way. I cared more about creating a worldly kingdom than seeking His first. It's not pretty, it's foolishness, but that is the truth. Remember, part of the purpose of the wilderness is to humble us and test our heart, my heart was full of avarice, coveting, greed, and that impaired me from seeking His kingdom first.

In Luke 12:15 God warns us, "Then he said to them, 'Watch out! Be on your guard against all kinds of greed; life does not consist in an abundance of possessions.'" (Luke 12:15 NIV) I understood this logically but I needed God to transform my heart like only He can.

All these months in the wilderness showed me what truly matters, and it's absolutely
His kingdom.

My heart finally understood it. Does that mean that I don't have to remind myself of that and let God remind me and rebuke me and course correct me? No! I am a flawed human and I need His power to overcome my flesh, the power of the Holy Spirit. The difference is that in the wilderness I truly understood, -not just logically. My heart understood. That's when I started seeking Him with all of my heart and that began true transformation in me and healing in my heart. God created us and he understands who we are better than we do ourselves. This is why true change requires God to change our hearts.

You may not have the same struggle, but we all have our own battles. Maybe the heart that God wants to examine is when it comes to other fleshly desires "Now the works of the flesh are obvious: sexual immorality, moral impurity, promiscuity, idolatry, sorcery, hatreds, strife, jealousy, outbursts of anger, selfish ambitions, dissentions, factions, envy, drunkenness, carousing, and anything similar. I am warning you about these things—as I warned you before—that those who practice such things will not inherit the kingdom of God." (Galatians 5:19-21 CSB) God literally warns us against these things because we will not inherit His kingdom, which is exactly the opposite of Matthew 6:33 to seek His kingdom first. Is there anything in your life that you need to recognize and ask God to help you remove?

This is not a matter of salvation, but a matter of living the abundant life in Christ on this earth, and being guided, and in fellowship with the Holy Spirit. It is about devoting your life to your Lord because you love Him above all else, because He loved us first. It is living in the awe and the fear of the Lord. Living a life well lived to say thank you and become more like Him throughout our life. Living righteously. The journey of sanctification cannot get started if we don't allow God to be the true Lord of our life in the full sense. And while the pruning hurts, it also gives new life and abundant fruit. Who wouldn't want to be fruitful for your Heavenly Father?

"Now those who belong to Christ Jesus have crucified the flesh with its passions and desires." (Galatians 5:24

CSB) When we fully surrender to our Lord, we are able to crucify the flesh because we belong to Him. Crucify our passions and desires! That's great to know. God has given us the power of the Holy Spirit who lives inside. The Living God is inside of us with power and might and strength.

So, can we crucify our passions? Of course! The Spirit will give us its fruit! The delicious fruit of living with the Holy Spirit. "But the fruit of the Spirit is love, joy, peace, patience, kindness, goodness, faithfulness, gentleness, and self-control..." (Galatians 5:22-23 CSB)

The Living God doesn't leave us alone in the wilderness. Instead, it is a time when we get to deep dive into our deepest matters of the heart so that God can be like a surgeon and remove what needs to be removed, to make us healthy even if the process is painful. The pruning process.

Lesson 2:

A Time of Revelation

Just as much as God doesn't leave us alone in the wilderness, he also reveals Himself to us in ways that can be new to us. There are always new aspects of God that we are getting to know throughout our life because He is God and all knowing. But it is like the wilderness is a catalyst to download much revelation unto us in deep ways.

This is what happened to me. During this time of wilderness, God really manifested Himself to me.
I was able to sense His Spirit so palpably, being with me. And the Word became alive like it had never before to me prior to this. I was seeking God with all of my heart!
I knew he was the only one who could rescue me from my pain. Not only did He heal my heart, but He gave me so much more as He always does. He gives more that we deserve and more that we even ask for. The peace beyond understanding that Philippians 4:7 talks about became alive "And the peace of God, which transcends all understanding, will guard your hearts

and your minds in Christ Jesus." (Philippians 4:7 NIV.) There is a verse previous to this one, "Do not be anxious about anything, but in every situation, by prayer and petition, with thanksgiving, present your requests to God." (Philippians 4:6 NIV.) When we go to God, our Father, and request a petition with a grateful heart even in the hardest circumstances, He is sure to listen and respond with His promise. Which is peace that doesn't make sense, when we are going through such hard moments, it is this peace that guards our heart and mind with Jesus as He promises us.

Since our heart and our mind is guarded by the peace that Jesus gives us, we are able to receive revelation. The wilderness empties us of ourselves and allows us to get filled with the Holy Spirit. Every time I would open His word, the Holy Spirit would reveal so much insight. I read the book of Daniel and actually understood what it was saying, even about the prophecies of the end times, something I had never been able to do before. I read 2 Samuel and Proverbs and Ecclesiastes, Mark, John, Acts, Romans, 1 Corinthians and Titus. It all became alive!

During this time, it wasn't that I had to become smarter or a Bible student, instead I became a friend of God. "The Lord is a friend to those who fear him. He teaches them his covenant." (Psalm 25:14 NLT) During this time, I understood that pure and true fear of the Lord is fearing being away from Him because you learn how to be in communion with Him. The Lord is a friend to those who fear Him, and He became my friend and my teacher.

The Lord will not leave you alone. He gives that peace beyond understanding. He draws near to you. He is your friend. Another translation for (Psalms 25:14) reads, "The secret counsel of the LORD is for those who fear him, and he reveals his covenant to them." (Psalms 25:14 *CSB*) It is clearly stated that He *reveals*. A time of revelation arises in the wilderness as this friendship forms deeper. And He begins to disclose his mysteries. Not that you have to go through a wilderness season to experience this but this is what happened for me.

I believe God knows how to open us up to receive revelation and some of us are just harder to get through.

I believe that the time of revelation comes because of the willingness of our hearts in this time. When we are stripped of our hard hearts. Just as the word of God tells us, that God hardened the heart of Pharaoh in (Exodus 7:3-4) "But I will harden Pharaoh's heart, and though I multiply my signs and wonders in the land of Egypt, Pharaoh will not listen to you .Then I will lay my hand on Egypt and bring my hosts, my people the children of Israel, out of the land of Egypt by great acts of judgment." (Exodus 7:3-4 ESV)

God also hardened the hearts of the people whom he had commanded Joshua to conquer. Joshua 11:20 says "For it was the LORD's intention to harden their hearts, so that they would engage Israel in battle, be completely destroyed without mercy, and be annihilated, just as the LORD had commanded Moses." (Joshua 11:20 CSB)

It seems cruel that God hardens the hearts of the people to destroy them. Doesn't it? However, God only responds to the state that their hearts were already in. God always gives us the free will to choose for ourselves how we want to respond. The only reason why He brought judgment on the Egyptians and on the conquered lands of the kings of the promised land was because there was no repentance or willingness to ask Him to be their God and LORD.

When we humble ourselves and have an open heart towards God and we seek Him with all of our heart we are doing the opposite of hardening our hearts, so God responds opposite of how He did to the people, in these passages.

He gives us a soft heart, willing and open to receive Him and everything of who He is. Therefore, He is able to reveal Himself to us in a deeper way because we are letting Him in. "Behold, I stand at the door and knock. If anyone hears my voice and opens the door, I will come in to him and eat with him, and he with me." (Revelation 3:20 ESV)

We *eat* with the Lord, we eat of His love, His mercy, His friendship, it is a close intimate encounter in which He reveals things to us as a friend would when eating a meal together. This is the promise He gives us; "And I will give you a new heart, and I will put in a new spirit in you, I will take out your stony, stubborn heart and give you a tender, responsive heart." (Ezekiel 36:26 NLT)

Lesson 3:

The Wilderness as a Time of Preparation and Character Building

It seems that the wilderness tends to begin with one main catastrophic event; then while you are there, there might be more events to accompany it. Like a two-for-one, but of things we don't want to go through. Yet, there are lessons to be learned or refused to learn through it. I once heard that you cannot shorten the time that God has set for you in the wilderness but you can surely lengthen it, but more on that later.

Let's just say that the death of our daughter was the earthquake size event that left us in the wilderness, but it wasn't the only event that was hard during this season of our life. There were also big financial issues we underwent shortly after her death. Then, there was the difficulty of navigating with my husband if we should try again for another baby. After we agreed to move forward on trying again, there was a long season of waiting to conceive that we hadn't previously experienced with our prior three pregnancies. More pruning, more pain. I was desperate to conceive right away, little did I know that my desperation and my husband's hesitation to ever try again, were just all part of the wilderness that we had to work through. All that to say is; do not be surprised if there are other challenges that arise once you are already deep in the wilderness.

But God will get you through those too. And there will be altars in the desert for you to remember those times, once you are out of the wilderness and into your promised land.

In the Book of Joshua, God instructs Joshua to tell the twelve leaders of the tribes of Israel to gather stones and set them up as an altar for the Lord before they enter the promised land so that they, and their future generations, can always remember what God did in the wilderness.

So that they wouldn't forget the lessons of the wilderness once they entered the promised land.

"and said to them, 'Go across to the ark of the LORD your God in the middle of the Jordan. Each of you lift a stone onto his shoulder, one for each of the Israelite tribes, so that this will be a sign among you. In the future, when your children ask you, "What do these stones mean to you?" you should tell them, "The water of the Jordan was cut off in front of the ark of the LORD's covenant. When it crossed the Jordan, the

Jordan's water was cut off." Therefore, these stones will always be a memorial for the Israelites."' (Joshua 4: 5-7 CSB)

This monument was set to remember how God miraculously got them out of the wilderness and into the promised land. This altar in the desert will be a symbol for you to remember the deliverance of God out of the wilderness season, out of your desert. You will be able to tell your future generations about how God delivered you from this place. You will remember these lessons, the pain, but you will have a new character! Hand delivered by your almighty God for you during this time. The character and the fruit that otherwise you would have not experienced. I know it's not pleasant to hear but we need time of suffering, time of pressure, time of refining to be better on the other side.

So how is our character built in the wilderness? I believe it is because we don't have true faith until it is tested. We don't know how strong we are, until we feel we are breaking. We don't desperately seek our God with all of our heart, until He is the only way we will get through it. The wilderness teaches us strength and resilience. It teaches us to keep going even if we feel we can't because we are not under our own strength, but *His*. And that's true character building. Praise God!

Could it be that God allows the wilderness season as an intense type of bootcamp preparation for another place, another season? Since the wilderness shapes our character so much, I do believe that it's a precursor that God allows and plans for so that we are able to face the next season. What follows a season of wilderness?

The Promised Land! Our promised land looks different for all of us, but it is a place and a season of breakthrough, abundance, and new beginnings. At the point in which we are ready for the promised land it's because the shaping of the wilderness has allowed us to become strong to fight the battles and to conquer in this new place.

We develop faith and obedience, first to hear God's voice, then to trust Him and obey it. Like when God told the Israelites the plan to conquer Jericho. It was not with military strategy, but with marching around following instructions and obeying even if it made no sense. You can read about Jericho in the book of Joshua chapter 6. The point is that the wilderness teaches us to practice obedience and patience as well.

The season of the wilderness after my daughter's death, was so much back and forth with God. Questioning why? Yet coming to the conclusion that He is God, I am not, and I need to trust Him. I need to trust Him in the things that I wish wouldn't have to happen. But

I also need to trust Him in the plans He has for me, and trust that His word is always true.

"For I know the plans I have for you'—this is the LORD's declaration— 'plans for your well-being, not for disaster, to give you a future and a hope." (Jeremiah 29:11 CSB) So if his plans are for good and not for disaster, that means that if we are in the middle of the wilderness in what feels like a disaster, it means he is not done with you yet!

If it's not good, He is not done yet! God has a way of restoring all things, and even if we think everything is lost as mere humans, remember his thoughts are higher than ours. "'For my thoughts are not your thoughts, and your ways are not my ways.' This is the LORD's declaration. 'For as heaven is higher than the earth, so my ways are higher than your ways, and my thoughts than your thoughts." (Isaiah 55: 8-9 CSB). Therefore, what we can't understand in our human mind which is limited, He already has a plan in his infinite wisdom and goodness.

Lesson 4

Can you Shorten your Wilderness?

I very much believe that you cannot shorten the season
of the wilderness because it is something that God has
set up for you individually. For a specific purpose and
time frame. It does not mean that God is angry with
you or that you fell into a sin that got you there. We
have to remember that this world is broken and
sometimes things just happen and God allows them to
happen to shape you in certain ways. What the enemy
meant for evil God uses it for good.

However, you can single handedly lengthen the
duration of a wilderness season by your actions or
response during this time of shaping. It wouldn't seem
rational that we would lengthen our season, it might
not even be what we want to hear, but it can happen in
various ways.

I believe that there are specific ways that we can
lengthen a wilderness season that God might have
intended for to be shorter. I want to go over some

examples from scripture to see how the Israelites lengthened their journey through the literal desert and how if we fall into these things we can do the same for ourselves. Of course, this is not an exhaustive list but there are still lessons to be learned.

There are instances of the Israelites complaining, disobeying, and having fear instead of faith. They wandered for forty years through the wilderness before they got into the promised land.

Complaining

The Israelites complained over and over about various things. The food, for one, on multiple occasions. "The entire Israelite community grumbled against Moses and Aaron in the wilderness. The Israelites said to them, 'If only we had died by the LORD's hand in the land of Egypt, when we sat by pots of meat and ate all the bread we wanted. Instead, you brought us into this wilderness to make this whole assembly die of hunger!'" (Exodus 16:2-3 CSB)

This lets us see the disagreeable state of the heart of the Israelites. Even after experiencing all the miracles that God did to free them, including parting the sea and killing the army behind them, they still complained. God had set them free from their place of slavery but all they were thinking about was the food they would eat as slaves and could no longer eat. The Israelites didn't consider or care that the meat they feasted on in Egypt, was the same meat that would have first been sacrificed to the gods of the Egyptians. And they didn't even care that they were enslaved while doing it. The Israelites were so entangled in the culture and with their masters in Egypt that they didn't care about sacrificing their convictions to feast on the abundance of Egypt.

Is this how we are? are we so entangled in the things of this world and the masters we hold dear that we would rather be slaves than to live in God's true freedom?
Do your Egyptian masters resemble food like it did in this instance, are you a slave to gluttony? How about sex in any way that is not God's design? How about living for money as your master, ambition, debt, envy, comparison, climbing the ladder at the cost of slavery? Or is your place of captivity different, are you a slave to the masters of anxiety? Depression? Worry? Fear?

Could it be that God has taken you through a desert season, a wilderness season so that you learn how not only to be out of Egypt, the land of your slavery, but actually learn how it looks to be free? Free from the things that bind us captive and away from the true freedom and life of purpose that God has for us.

The wilderness is this transition period of your past slavery and God's training for where you are supposed to be. The promised land! Your purpose in God's kingdom and how your life is meant to be versus what it is when you are a slave.

It is so difficult for us to die to ourselves and our past when it comes to the things that made us comfortable. The Israelites craved to be back in the place of comfort for them which provided food that they didn't have in the desert. The Bible is strong in the descriptive language of the type of people who craved food other than manna. It was the scum of the Israelites, the ungrateful and foolish. "The riffraff among them had a strong craving for other food. The Israelites wept again and said, 'Who will feed us meat? We remember the free fish we ate in Egypt, along with the cucumbers, melons, leeks, onions, and garlic. But now our appetite is gone; there's nothing to look at but this manna!'" (Numbers 11:4-6 CSB)

When God provides something that sustains us in the wilderness, what do we miss from the place of our slavery? Is it our old sin of what we used to do and how fun it was and how good it tasted? The pleasures of life that kept us captive? We have to be real with ourselves and examine our hearts because until our hearts change, we will be stuck in the wilderness eating manna just surviving but never truly being satisfied or thriving.

Remember that God didn't want them to live off of manna their whole life, it was not ideal, His plan was the promised land. We keep ourselves out of our promised land with our own bondages. The flaws of the human condition are easier to detect in others than ourselves. We can read this and realize that the "free fish" that they ate along with all the other things was not free at all. It was paid by a life of slavery. Being controlled by someone else, along with all their family and their generations. Exhausting work, no free choice and a defeated spirit seems like a very high price to pay for "free fish" and other delectable things.

Disobedience

What else did the Israelites do in the wilderness to lengthen it? Let's look at how disobedient they were. What God asked of them, versus what they actually did?

God gave them some instructions, as He does to all of us, and it's up to us to be obedient. "Then the Lord said to Moses, 'I am going to rain bread from heaven for you. The people are to go out each day and gather enough for the day. This way I will test them to see whether or not they will follow my instructions'" (Exodus 16:4 CSB) God is explicitly saying that these instructions are to test them to see if they will follow them. He wanted them to obey Him and trust that He would be their provider each day as He still wants us to trust and obey Him today.

The people had had such trouble following these simple instructions to gather just enough for the day. Some gathered more than the allotted amount for each person. Some wanted to save it for the next day, when God clearly said it was only for that day. Some wanted to gather and make it on Sabbath even though God instructed them to gather twice as much on the sixth day so it would be enough for Sabbath. God often reminds us to only worry about the day, not the next or the next "Therefore don't worry about tomorrow, because tomorrow will worry about itself. Each day has enough trouble of its own." (Matthew 6:34 CSB).

Clearly the Israelites at this point didn't know how to follow instructions given by God, they hadn't developed the obedience that they needed to acquire the promise land God already had for them.

This is why their disobedience lengthened their time in the desert. Since God knew they would not be ready to follow his instructions on anything else. Like on how to take possession of the land, battle strategies, where to settle, etc. It was clear they needed more time of refinement in the wilderness and so can we.

That's the process of the wilderness. It shapes our character for obedience so that when we are ready, we can enter the promised land and obey the Lord's instruction. When new instructions come, our heart will be willing and ready to obey. Such as the Israelites, led by Joshua, had to obey the instructions to march around Jericho in silence for six days and then blow the trumpets on the seventh day and take the city. "Early on the seventh day, they started at dawn and marched around the city seven times in the same way. That was the only day they marched around the city seven times. After the seventh time, the priests blew the rams' horns, and Joshua said to the troops, 'Shout! For the LORD has given you the city.'" (Joshua 6:15- 16 CSB) This battle strategy made no sense logically as a military strategy but that didn't matter. What mattered was their obedience to God's instructions and God delivered them the city, and they entered the promised land.

Obedience wasn't always the case in the promised land, as we see right after when they were defeated at Ai as we read in Joshua chapter 7 "The Israelites, however, were unfaithful regarding the things set apart for destruction. Achan, son of Carmi, son of Zabdi, son of Zerah, of the tribe of Judah, took some of what was set apart, and the LORD's anger burned against the Israelites." (Joshua 7:1 CBS)

That was another lesson they had to learn by the death of this unfaithful man and his family. The sad part is that we can judge others so easily for their unfaithfulness to God when it comes to the things that are easy for us to obey, but can we look at ourselves and understand there are areas of unfaithfulness that we have to work on? The ones that are hard for us and we don't even want others to know about. The ones that we can even justify and keep doing because the grace of God covers us? Yes, God is always good. And yes, His grace never ends which is why Jesus gave his life for us, but is that how you want to live? In bondage to sin and back to the slavery he pulled us out of?

That doesn't seem like a way to honor the sacrifice of Jesus, the life we choose to live should strive for obedience, holiness, the fear of the Lord because we are set apart for him and the way we live our life is a thank you for his sacrifice out of the love we have for Him, because He loved us first when we were still sinners.

No, works don't earn us salvation. Grace is a free gift, but God deserves glory and honor and obedience and faithfulness. This draws us deeper with God. If we have the fear of God, the fear of being distant from him because of perpetual reoccurring sin, then we choose to live differently.

As the apostle Paul wrote in Philippians "Therefore, my dear friends, just as you have always obeyed, so now, not only in my presence but even more in my absence, work out your own salvation with fear and trembling." (Philippians 2:12 CSB). If we live with the fear of God, this is the awe and reverence for God. It is recognizing God's holiness versus our sinful nature which is why we should continue to grow in our faith and commitment to Jesus.

This, my friends, is sanctification, an ongoing process for us to be more like our Lord, and it will not be done until the day of salvation. This only happens by God's refinement through the fire, the wilderness of life, and how we respond to it. Let's not elongate our wilderness, instead respond in excellence. Not in disobedience, and faithlessness but with obedience and faith. The awe of God, if understood in our heart, makes us want to respond to Him in these ways.

The Israelites also chose disobedience about worshiping false gods and dishonored God's exclusive covenant with them. God warned them multiple times against worship of false gods.

In Exodus 20 where the ten commandments are established. "Do not have other gods besides me. Do not make an idol for yourself, whether in the shape of anything in the heavens above or on the earth below or in the waters under the earth. Do not bow in worship to them, and do not serve them; for I, the LORD your God, am a jealous God, bringing the consequences of the fathers' iniquity on the children to the third and fourth generations of those who hate me, but showing faithful love to a thousand generations of those who love me and keep my commands." (Exodus 20: 3-6 CSB)

Also, in Exodus 34 where God talks about the covenant and obeying its obligations "Because the LORD is jealous for his reputation you are never to bow down to another god. He is a jealous God." (Exodus 34:14) Then God reminds them again and Deuteronomy 5 before entering the promised land. "I am the LORD your God, who brought you out of the land of Egypt, out of the place of slavery. Do not have other gods besides me. Do not make an idol for yourself in the shape of anything in the heavens above or on the earth below or in the waters under the earth. Do not bow in worship to them, and do not serve them, because I, the LORD your God, am a jealous God, bringing the consequences of the fathers' iniquity on the children to the third and fourth generations of those who hate me, but showing faithful love to a thousand generations of those who love me and keep my commands." (Deuteronomy 5:6-10 CSB)

God repeats to us what is important again and again because we are like little kids who need reminders to learn things until we truly learn them.

There were various instances in which the Israelites worshipped gods again and again. How does this relate to us?

I think we aren't really worshiping carved images or golden calves these days. However, we do worship the gods of success in whatever shape that represents for us; whether it be financial, educational, fame, power, influence etc. What if it's the god of ourselves, doing our own will instead of the will of God in our lives and living however we please?

Remember that anything we choose to put in the place of God is worshiping false gods. This is even in things that are good such as our spouse, children or even vocational ministry, if they are in first place, they are taking the place that only belongs to God. That really hurts because I think most of us have done it in one sense or another. In the wilderness, there is a time to choose if we are going to worship any of the false gods that entice us.

Fear over Faith

When we are getting refined by fire in this hard season will we choose anxiety, worry, fear? Or will our faith remain with the one and only true God and know that he has it under control. That if it is not good yet, he is not done with it. He is not done with you!

Remain faithful in the wilderness, do not get impatient and worship false gods, do not get disobedient. Instead abide in Him. He promises to be close to the brokenhearted and those crushed in spirit "The LORD is close to the brokenhearted and saves those who are crushed in spirit." (Psalm 34:18 NIV)

The Lord will never leave you nor forsake you, so abide in Him. You are passing through this wilderness; you will not stay here forever. Don't elongate it. This will pass. God has a plan for you on the other side.

How do we keep the faith and not give way to fear in the time of the wilderness?

The reason why fear is so bad as believers is because it is the opposite of faith. It is the opposite of trusting God, satan loves to intimidate us with his lies and he implants fear in us. With his whispering, or rather yelling of "you're never getting out of this place, this is your life now. How can anything good come out of this? You're just going to keep going through this bad stuff. God doesn't love you. God doesn't see you. You are bad and God is punishing you!"
The devil is a liar and Jesus explicitly tells us this in John 8 "Why don't you understand what I say? Because you cannot listen to my word. You are of your father the devil, and you want to carry out your father's desires. He was a murderer from the beginning and does not stand in the truth, because there is no truth in him. When he tells a lie, he speaks from his own nature, because he is a liar and the father of lies." (John 8:43-44 CSB)

If God is not your father, then the devil is your father and that's such a hard statement to read, but this is why we put our faith in Jesus. He is incapable of telling lies because He is truth, just as the devil is incapable of telling the truth because he is the father of lies.

This reminds me of when Joshua gave the people choices of who they would serve before entering the promised land but he boldly declares "But as for me and my house, we will serve the LORD." (Joshua 24:15) After a long period of being in the wilderness right before God is getting us ready to enter the promised land, we have to make the choice too, who will we serve? Faith or Fear? God or the devil?

The wilderness is a time in which we have a lot of time to reflect on how we are walking with God. We can choose to have faith and live by faith despite our circumstances or we can choose to listen to the devil and the spirit of fear and intimidation and we will be doing the opposite. This is why living in fear is a way to elongate the period of the wilderness. It is a matter of the heart just as a lot of things are.

Of course, when we are walking in the wilderness it is hard for our human nature not to experience fear. At every corner it is lingering. This is when we draw from the well of faith and eradicate the fear knowing that "the one who is in you is greater than the one who is in the world." (1 John 4:4 CSB)

The Spirit of God who lives in us as believers is greater than the spirit of the world, of the flesh, which is satan.

So, when you feel like you can't go any further in the wilderness season remember that the Spirit of God lives inside of you. He empowers us with his Holy Spirit and we can make it through anything because we are not doing it alone. When you are tempted to have fear, cast it away from you and declare who you belong to and the faith you have placed in your Lord and Savior Jesus who is your Redeemer and will take you out of the wilderness in its due time.

Lesson 5:

Manna is For the Wilderness Not the Promise Land

"He fed you in the wilderness with manna, which your ancestors had not known, in order to humble and test you, so that in the end he might cause you to prosper." (Deuteronomy 8:16 CSB)

Manna is part of the sustenance that God gives to us while we are in the wilderness. But it is just that, we survive with it but it is not the plan that He has for us out of the wilderness. He doesn't let us starve because He will always be our provider, Jehovah-Jireh, but remember that the manna is also to humble us and test us.

How do we react in the wilderness when we are barely surviving? Emotionally, do we go off on people, or do we remain kind as we are walking with only the manna from our wilderness and we see others eating choice food because they can be in a different season? It's ok to not be thriving in the difficult season of the wilderness. But we do have to remember that God will always make a way for us even if it's not the preferred way that we would have chosen. The good news is that even though this is a difficult season, let's take God's word for what it is and take in the whole truth.

The whole truth is that He will prosper us at the end. It is written right there alongside the difficult truth. So yes, the wilderness is difficult but God doesn't want us to stay there. That's why I say the manna is only temporary. Christ came to give us life in abundance. (John 10:10) And we hang on to that truth.

Can we still be loving to others around us? Especially the ones closest to us, as we sometimes have to pour out of an empty cup.

We shouldn't always have to do this, but we should do it while it is necessary for survival in this season. When our daughter died, I had to make a decision that would not only affect the time in the wilderness but also my descendants and future generations.
What type of mom would my two sons, who were well and alive, going to have? Would my precious little boys have a shell of a woman who stays in the wilderness forever, as a mom? Or would they have a mom who extracted all of the nourishment presented from manna in the wilderness. Meaning, someone who kept living and growing and knowing that somehow the wilderness would have an end because of who God is.

I chose the latter, and God honored that decision and got me through the wilderness.

See, we don't do things in our own strength. We can't! But when we choose something that aligns with the will of God, He empowers us with his Holy Spirit to see us complete it. Doesn't mean that I didn't have overwhelming sadness in my heart, and questions, and that I wept a lot. But my sons remained as an absolute gift in the wilderness, like an oasis of refreshing water and joy in the time of sorrow in the desert. So, I knew I had to treat them as such, and I hope I did.
I guess I won't find out until they are adults and we can talk about how they experienced this season in their life from their own perspective of losing their sister.

We all navigated together as a family, not by pretending we weren't going through a hard time but by understanding that we were doing it together and God was guiding us. His word gives us instruction on what to think about in Philippians 4:8 and to look for the good things in life.

We all have good things and we need to contemplate them and think about them a lot because it is so helpful. No matter how difficult the season is, we all have good things to focus on and dwell in.
"And now, dear brothers and sisters, one final thing. Fix your thoughts on what is true, and honorable, and right, and pure, and lovely, and admirable. Think about

things that are excellent and worthy of praise."
(Philippians 4:8)

What does this mean? That we make the conscious
choice to think about these things, meditate on them
because they bring life. And when you live this out, the
wilderness becomes less terrifying. This is the renewing
of our mind and we don't conform to the patterns of
this world. (Romans 12:2) We don't ruminate on the
negative and the sad and give way to fear, but we live
by faith and the beauty that is always present because
we have God.

The promises of the future are also fuel in the
wilderness. God promised to bring you into a good
land where you will have plenty and lack nothing.
(Deuteronomy 8:9) So keep looking ahead in the
wilderness and don't lose sight that you will not be
there forever. God will bring you out of it into a good
land! The abundance of the promised land will come.

Lesson 6:

Navigating the Wilderness as If it Was an Earthquake.

I completely owe this lesson to the wisdom God gave to my husband in this season.

My husband took the leadership as the head of the household that God gave to him and he was such a rock in this season of facing the death of our daughter. Even though he was going through the same thing, he put his needs second and wanted to make sure that I was okay as his wife and that our kids were okay dealing with the loss of their sister.

It was a long and emotional process which happened in steps. He later described it to me as navigating through an earthquake. We live in Southern California and grew up having earthquakes, so they are very familiar to us. The way he explained it was, that there is an initial shock, which tends to be the biggest and does the destruction if it's big enough. Then there are aftershocks which can also cause destruction. Then there is a reconstruction process. So, let's talk about how that looks when you are going through a season of struggle.

The Earthquake

The earthquake can be anything that you go through that's very difficult. A divorce, a loss of a job, a life-changing accident, the death of a loved one, a devastating diagnosis, etc. When this big event happens, you are in shock, you can't even believe what just happened sometimes and you are just covering yourself and hanging on for dear life, almost as a survival instinct.

When the earthquake is happening, the first instinct is to make sure your family is okay. More than likely, you would check on everyone if they are in proximity to you or call whoever you need to call. That's what happens in these circumstances of life. That's the approach that my husband took when we went through our earthquake.

He wanted to make sure that me and our boys were okay. How was I doing, especially with being postpartum and recovering physically and navigating through this big loss with hormones running through my body? How are the kids doing, have we talked to them enough for them to even comprehend what was happening since they were only eight and five years old?

We developed a plan to make sure we would maintain a routine for them to give them a sense of security. We had extensive and repeated conversations to address their feelings no matter what they were and make clear to them that they were able to talk about anything with us. Then making sure they felt loved and certain that we would get through this as a family because God was carrying us through this. We also got professional help as an added assurance that they were okay. All of this was the initial reactions after the big earthquake event.

The Aftershocks

Then came the aftershocks! These are hard, they seem subtle but can be so harmful. It's like when the big earthquake happens and then everything stops shaking and you feel a sense of relief but it doesn't mean there are no cracks in the wall that seem harmless but can be absolutely devastating with an aftershock. The crack can end up destroying a full wall or ceiling that weakens the structural integrity of the whole building. That's what can happen emotionally and spiritually as well. These aftershocks were hard to deal with.

It was asking why, and many other questions? The anger towards God, then the pleading for forgiveness of the anger. Then the confusion of wondering why over and over again. Then the guessing game and guilt of trying to figure out if this was my fault? Was it past sin I was paying for? Was it carelessness, and that somehow, I put my baby in danger by doing something, or not doing something during the pregnancy.

Then digging into the word for answers and realizing that I might never get them on this side of eternity and accepting that. At the end of the day God's thoughts are higher than our thoughts and his ways higher than our ways just as heaven is higher than earth. (Isaiah 55:8-9) Knowing this and accepting this truth still didn't alleviate all my human emotions because it would take time for God to fully heal my heart. But it did give me the truth and the fact that I had to accept this as truth because I am not God and although I didn't understand I had to submit to His will and not give into my pride.

You have to be careful with these aftershocks because if you leave them unattended, they can destroy the building, and they can destroy your emotional wellbeing and even shake your faith. You have to stand firm on the rock who is Jesus when these questions come.

The cracks kept appearing. Every day when I would take my boys to school and then I would have to go home empty-handed after thinking that I would be taking a baby with me. That was a huge crack but God held my hand as we patched it all up. Through all my lows, and all my doubts. There was always repentance and full surrender after. Moments of doubt, followed by moments of praise. He is patient with us as we go through this. He is not a distant God, but our God knows what it is to be human as He came and humbled Himself into the lowly position after leaving His throne to serve us. Even though He was there at the creation of the universe, He still chose to come and save us.

So how can we think that He will not rescue us from our wilderness? He will.

Today as I sit here writing this, I am 30 weeks pregnant with my son, my redemption story. My gift from above. I can go into labor at any moment and I need to absolutely trust God that it is indeed my redemption story and not another earthquake. I guess even now, 1.5 years after the earthquake, I still experience the aftershocks. But guess what?

My God is here with me. As the tears pour out in this moment the fear dissipates because I remember the journey He has taken me on. The Journey of the Wilderness has not been wasted. God never wastes pain, and He will not waste yours either. He is there with you whether you are in the middle of the shaking or in the aftershocks or even at the reconstruction side and wondering what direction to take. God has got us

The Reconstruction

All I can say about the reconstruction process is that it needs to be God driven to set strong foundations and a stronger building for the next season. Only God can guide you and direct you to the next season after the wilderness. Only God can guide you to what it will look like for you. As for me, and my household we will serve the Lord (Joshua 24:15) and He will show me the way to the promised land.

Some time passed from when I last wrote, when I wasn't sure if my son would be my redemption story or another horrible wilderness.

I can say with great rejoicing that God has allowed me to receive my gift and enter into a different season. Not of wilderness, but of the promised land, a season of hope that He will also deliver to you.

My son is perfectly healthy and has been an amazing reminder of God's goodness. He is not even done with my story yet and He is not done with your story yet. In this next season, the life of my baby boy into this world is a part of my story.

There is hope after the wilderness and I get to write in very real time with very real emotions about the journey. He is a reminder of the goodness and faithfulness of God. The mourning turned to rejoicing.

I praise God for my son's life so much and even more so because of the wilderness I was in and then got out of. The wilderness creates a way to appreciate the good things like nothing else can.

God has a plan of reconstruction for everyone who walks with Him and calls out His name in the middle of the earthquake. God is not done with you. No matter how dark things seem right now, God will always use it for good, even what seems so horrible. Remember Romans 8:28 "We know that all things work together for the good of those who love God, who are called according to his purpose." (Romans 8:28 CSB) Yes, this means *all things*, including the good and the bad, but it is all part of the reconstruction process God will do in your life.

To plan a reconstruction project after a big earthquake, you can't just do it on your own. You would need architects, engineers, contractors, a labor force, and so many others.

To plan a reconstruction of your life after a devastating event you need God above all. You and Him spending time one on one and Him speaking into your life. Carve out time to connect with your Heavenly Father, and He will guide you along the right path. "The LORD says, 'I will guide you along the best pathway for your life. I will advise you and watch over you.'" (Psalms 32:8 NLT). It is written in His word, and He will do exactly that. He can also guide you to rely on your family, friends, community, and professional help to get you over this wilderness but seek Him first so He can direct you.

Lesson 7:

Priorities

One thing that a hard situation is sure to do is make you realize the true priorities of your life. You will quickly realize, maybe for some of us not so quickly, how out of order we place importance on things.

We dedicate a lot of our time, energy, and mind, to things that at the end are not as important as we think. Since the wilderness humbles us, it teaches us to align our priorities better. "Remember that the LORD your God led you on the entire journey these forty years in the wilderness, so that he might humble you and test you to know what was in your heart, whether or not you would keep his commands. He humbled you by letting you go hungry; then he gave you manna to eat… so that you might learn that man does not live on bread alone but every word that comes from the mouth of the LORD." (Deuteronomy 8: 2-3 CSB)

When we realize that even though we need food to nourish our physical bodies, that's not as important as the word of God. Just as we need water, we need the living water of God even more. Meaning, that we place so much importance on the things of the flesh, more so than the things of the Spirit, a lot of the time. And we tend to get our priorities of the things that truly matter out of order.

When we struggle to see life in the way that God meant for us to live it, the wilderness shows us.

We saw this when the world stopped during the covid pandemic. Once we couldn't go to any places, whether to work or study or eat out or any other entertainment, we realized that who is in our home and in our hearts is the most important. Family and friends; your spouse, your children, your parents, siblings, your church community and friends.

It's easy to take even the people we love the most for granted in the pursuit of worldly goals, pleasures, disciplines. Not that those things are wrong as long as they are moral and not harmful, but the order of importance is what matters.

How do they stack up in our hearts? Do we truly give God the first place, our full love, with all of our hearts, soul and our mind?

"He said to him, 'Love the Lord your God with all of your heart, with all of your soul, and with all of your mind.'" (Matthew 22:37 CSB) Then do we give the people around us second place? "The second is like it; Love your neighbor as yourself." (Matthew 22:39 CSB) Then after God is in first, and the people around us in second, the rest follows after that. The career, the hustle for success, the entertainment, the vacations, the self-care, the hobbies, and all the other things that pull us into a lot of different directions. Not have all these things consume us and give the remainder to people and God.

And if we are to love our neighbor as ourselves, we should prioritize others, first our immediate family and then those around us, around our neighborhoods, and around the world.

Wilderness seasons also let us see who is really a close relationship to you, who you can count on and who can count on you. Outer and inner reflection. Love people and use things not the other way around, basically. When everything gets stripped back in the wilderness, it lets you assess if this is true of your life.

Lesson 8:

God Gives Peace That the World Cannot Steal

The wilderness is a place of hardship, yes. It is a place of character building, yes. It is a place of testing of your heart, yes. It is a place of refinement by the fire, yes.

But it is also a place in which no matter what's going on around you, no matter the circumstances, or the grieving, or the loss you might be experiencing, it is a place in which the Lord gives you peace that the world cannot steal.

"Peace I leave with you. My peace I give to you. I do not give to you as the world gives." (John 14:27 CSB)

Jesus specifically is giving us as believers his own peace that the world cannot give. He makes a differentiation of the peace of Jesus versus the peace of the world.

That's exactly what you get during the time of need in the wilderness. It is a time of peace even with trouble surrounding you because it doesn't depend on circumstances but on who God is.

The never changing God we serve. You can still have peace because it's not conditional. His word says his peace is beyond understanding. "And the peace of God, which surpasses all understanding, will guard your hearts and minds in Christ Jesus" (Philippians 4:7 CSB) Thank God that we are able to experience this in a wilderness season. It's another way of how our God takes care of us.

Lesson 9:

Choose Perseverance

In this world we will have trouble is a promise from God, "I have told you these things, so that in me you may have peace. In this world you will have trouble. But take heart! I have overcome the world." (John 16:33 NIV) There's that *peace* again.

So even though we will have trouble we can choose to have perseverance because we know that God has overcome the world and this gives us peace. No matter how many times we fall, we can get back up because we are holding on to God's hand and he lifts us up when life throws us around.

"Therefore, since we have been justified by faith, we have peace with God through our Lord Jesus Christ. We have also obtained access through him by faith into this grace in which we stand, and we boast in the hope of the glory of God. And not only that, but we also boast in our afflictions, because we know that affliction produces endurance, endurance produces proven character, and proven character produces hope. This hope will not disappoint us, because God's love has been poured out of our hearts through the Holy Spirit who was given to us." (Romans 5:1-5 CSB)

What do we get from our wilderness?

We get endurance, character, and hope. It is a decision that we take to anchor ourselves on Jesus and persevere because at the end of the day we know that even though we have troubles now, He has overcome the world. These trials will pass. We have the ultimate hope of eternity. He has overcome even the sting of death, and one day we will get to spend eternity with Him.

Therefore, choose this day to persevere and He will take you to the other side of your wilderness. He will make a way. He will always make a way. Persevere, and then not even the biggest earthquake can shake you down.

Lesson 10:

What Happens After the Wilderness?

Our Father who knows how He made us each individually, uniquely and wonderfully made knows us profoundly. Our creator is also our Heavenly Father and He wants the best for us. We know that as Romans 8:28 tells us "We know that all things work together for the good of those who love God, who are called according to his purpose." (Romans 8:28 CSB)

What works together? ALL things. For who? For those who love God and are called according to HIS purpose.

This became my favorite verse during this season because it gave me hope in the wilderness. It tells us what follows after a wilderness season, that no matter how hard something is, it will be good at the end. In the wilderness, the choice is yours, will you run away from God in anger or will you allow Him to embrace you, and will your love grow for Him as you connect more profoundly to your heavenly Father.

Look at the scripture again. Everything, all things, work out for those who love God. This is because He has us in the palm of His hand as His children and He is taking care of us because we love Him because He first loved us.

So, I ask myself, what was the purpose of the very short two-day life that my daughter got to live here on earth, and that we got to experience living with her?

Her life was only for such a short time but a forever impact. Her life brought us so many things. Her name, Elah, Is the Hebrew name for the terebinth tree mentioned in the Bible many times. A tree has seeds, but only if the seed dies will it produce many others.

This can be found in John 12:24 in which Jesus states "Very truly I tell you, unless a kernel of wheat falls to the ground and dies, it remains only a single seed. But if it dies, it produces many seeds." (John 12:24 NIV) God showed my husband and I this verse when I was still pregnant with her and we were researching what Elah meant, which is the name that God put in my husband's heart for us to name our daughter. When we read this verse, we didn't imagine all the sorrow that we would have to endure, we never thought that she would be the seed that would die to produce a lot of other seeds. So, what did her life produce?

It left her dad and I in the wilderness and produced all the lessons I talked about. It made us grow in our relationship with each other, God and our other children, including the one who came after her.

Our baby boy Mark is crying in the other room because he woke up from his nap as I write this and is about to be 2 months old.

After the wilderness there is hope, growth, new life. With God, all things are possible, and after your wilderness you too will find new seeds of life in your life. I can't wait to see everything else that God has in store for my family and I after the wilderness. After the refining, comes the rebuilding, and the promised land where more battles are fought but is also filled with milk and honey and every delicious food imaginable that will nourish you. The promised land is in sight for you too, God is with you.

We hope you have enjoyed this book,
May it help you and
Encourage you!

Don't Forget to write us a review and
Recommend this to a friend